PAULINE FLICK

Discovering
Toys and Toy
Museums

SHIRE PUBLICATIONS LTD

To Joan Cope

ACKNOWLEDGEMENTS

I should like to thank the many museum curators, toy manufacturers and private collectors who have helped me in the preparation of this book. I am especially grateful to Mr John Burrows for the photograph of the dolls' house in plate 24, to Mrs Betty Cadbury for plate 23, to Dean's Rag Book Company Ltd for plate 26, to Mr P. J. C. Harbutt for plate 25, to Mrs Vera Kramer for plate 19, and to Mr Gerald Whiting of the John Lewis Partnership for plate 18.

The following have also been kind enough to give permission for their photographs to be reproduced: the British Museum, plate 1; the Germanisches Nationalmuseum, Nuremberg, plate 2; the Victoria and Albert Museum, plates 3, 4, 5, 6, 8, 15; the Science Museum, plates 10, 11; the Public Record Office, plate 9; the Museum of Curiosity, Arundel, plate 14; Elizabethan House, Totnes, plate 16; Stockport Museum, plate 17; *Woman's Realm*, plate 21; Saffron Walden Museum, plate 22; and Worcester Museum, plate 27. The photographs in plates 28 and 29 were originally taken for *Country Life* by Mr Alex Starkey.

THE HISTORY OF TOYS

Many books have already been written about toys, for the subject is virtually inexhaustible. Most enthusiasts will have these books on their shelves, if not on their coffee tables, and it would be pointless, even if it were possible, to repeat here all of the detailed information they give. Every toy historian owes a great debt of gratitude to Karl Grober, the German author of *Children's Toys of Bygone Days;* the English edition was first published in 1928, and although it is unfortunately now out of print it can be consulted in many public libraries. Other useful works published more recently are listed in the bibliography at the end of this book. Meanwhile, this is an attempt first to give some idea of the playthings—large and small, cheap and costly, hand-made and mass-produced—that have been saved up for, played with and cherished by English children over the last three hundred years or so, and then to provide a guide to the many museums where they can be discovered and enjoyed.

Since all children instinctively try to copy adult behaviour and occupations the vast majority of toys have always been inspired by this universal wish to imitate grown-ups. The most obvious example is the little girl with her doll and all its various accessories, but miniature farm animals, soldiers, cars and now spacecraft are all part of the same unchanging pattern. Nobody knows when children first made mud pies, sailed pieces of bark, or realised that acorn cups were perfect miniature drinking vessels, but such improvisations must be nearly as old as civilisation itself. As for the deliberately constructed toy—the artifact created solely as a plaything—its early history is hardly less obscure, and almost nothing is known of any toys before those of the Ancient Egyptians.

Toys in Ancient Times

As early as 2000 B.C. wooden ship models and tableaux illustrating brewing, baking and other domestic occupations were being made in Egypt. These charming and colourful objects, so toy-like to our eyes, were however not playthings but funerary offerings, placed in tombs to help the dead in their journey to the next world. Undisturbed for centuries, they have survived intact in a way no toy could ever be expected to do, and some beautiful examples are on show in the British Museum. Although it is tempting to speculate that a civilisation capable of inspiring such lively miniatures probably produced other small things for children's amusement, the first true toys to have been preserved date from about a thousand years later. The British Museum's collection includes a wooden tiger with string-operated movable jaws (plate 1), a leg-less cow and some balls made of papyrus. They are not very spectacular, but considering the chances against their surviving at all we should perhaps make the same allowance as Dr. Johnson did for the performing dog.

Far more is known about the toys of Greek and Roman children. Contemporary literature, decorated vases and archaeological excavations combine to show that amongst other things they had clay rattles, jointed clay dolls, handcarts, hobby-horses, miniature pieces of furniture, balls and yoyos. Grober mentions that early Greek tourists visiting Troy could buy model Trojan horses as souvenirs, apparently complete with soldiers inside, and pre-dating the Noah's ark by two thousand years.

When they grew up it was certainly the custom for Greek girls to offer their dolls to the goddess Artemis, and boys their hoops and tops to Hermes, so obviously toys were an established feature of everyday life. The British Museum has a small terra-cotta group (c. 300 B.C.) of two girls playing knucklebones, and games of this sort were probably played as much by adults as by children. The Romans even had rag dolls; one was found in a child's grave, and this sad little relic too has found its way to Bloomsbury.

The Middle Ages

One might suppose that toys evolved continuously from these promising beginnings, but in fact they did nothing of the kind. Toy-making flourishes only in the context of a settled way of life, where houses have space for playthings to be kept, and where there is leisure and time enough for them to be enjoyed. Most important of all, society must have an indulgent attitude towards childhood. Life for affluent Egyptians, Greeks and Romans was sufficiently well-ordered for this luxury, but in the Dark Ages which followed the collapse of the Roman Empire, and in the Middle Ages to a lesser degree, existence was too unsettled and precarious for children to be given much special consideration. Almost as soon as a little boy or girl was old enough to play he or she would have been old enough to learn to handle weapons, tools, distaff or spinning wheel; in any case, the complete lack of mass-production techniques and the difficulties of communications and transport would have made it hard to lay hands on even the barest necessities, let alone non-essentials like toys. A very few mediaeval illuminated manuscripts show simple playthings such as tops, hobby-horses, balls and wind-mills—much the same sort of thing as the Greeks had, in fact. Anything more elaborate would have been only for the very rich, like the magnificent model soldiers given to young German princelings—as much to prepare them for war, one suspects, as to amuse them.

Peter Bruegel's well-known picture *Children's Games* is often cited to show how many toys children had in the sixteenth century, but although a close look reveals plenty of boisterous *games* there are not many real *toys*. Such as there are are mostly of the hoop/ball/top variety, and still a world away from the marvels which were to explode so brilliantly upon the nurseries of two and three hundred years later.

Early German wooden toys

However, the seeds of the German toy industry were sown quite early in the Middle Ages, and since Germany was to play such an outstanding part in the world's toy trade it is worth pausing to consider how it all began. Carving came naturally to a peasant community surrounded by dense forests, and South Germany in particular had a long tradition of making religious figures, especially for Christmas cribs. During the long winters there was not much work which could be

Nineteenth century German wooden toy with mechanical 'pecking hens'.

5

done on the farms, and the peasants filled in their time, and probably earned a little extra money, by carving simple household utensils and small playthings. At first the trade was purely local; the cost of transporting such intrinsically value-less goods in any quantity would have been prohibitive, but as time went on and communications improved these German toys found their way all over Europe and beyond. Merchants and other travellers, many of them on their way to the great fair at Leipzig, were only too pleased to buy the various local products to take home with them, and by the early sixteenth century a definite pattern of toy-trading had emerged. The workers came to be strictly organised under the guild system, which prevented, say, a wood turner from trespassing on the craft of a painter or decorator of wooden goods—a system which will readily be understood by anyone familiar with some of today's trade union practices. Because of its position, Nuremberg was already recognised as an international marketing centre for all sorts of goods, and soon the neighbouring districts specialising in toy-making—Oberammergau, the Groden Valley, Berchtesgaden and Sonneberg—were sending their wares there to be handled by experienced agents. Several book illustrations and portraits of the sixteenth and seventeenth centuries show dolls, dolls' beds, kites, windmills, stilts and the ubiquitous hobby-horse, but since most of these toys were made of wood and were therefore highly perishable it is too much to hope that more than a very few have been preserved.

It is difficult to say how many of these early German toys reached England. Simple toys of one kind or another were certainly carried round this country by hawkers and pedlars, and offered for sale at the many fairs held in most towns at regular intervals; but these might well have been made in quite small numbers at home, either by the pedlar himself or members of his family, in much the same way as gipsies still make clothes pegs and paper flowers. Ben Jonson, writing in 1614, mentions hobby-horses, gingerbread figures, miniature animals, dolls, fiddles and drums among the playthings to be bought at Smithfield's Bartholomew Fair, and it seems likely that some of these toys were imported—certainly there was no question of their production being organised here on any significant scale.

The eighteenth century

About the middle of the eighteenth century, though, a completely new era dawned for English children. Until now they had been regarded to all intents and purposes as miniature grown-ups, dressed in stiff adult clothing and expected to occupy themselves exclusively with learning and hard work in preparation for later life; the whole concept of play for its own sake was utterly foreign to a society still very much influenced by Puritan ideals. Even Dr. Isaac Watts, who was devoted to children and is generally considered to have been a model of tolerance, was careful to warn his little pupils not to grow too fond of games. *Divine and Moral Songs,* first published in 1715 and an immediate best-seller, includes the following 'Child's Complaint'

> *Why should I love my sport so well,*
> *So constant at my play;*
> *And lose the thoughts of heaven and hell,*
> *And then forget to pray?*

But verses like this were in themselves a great advance on the ranting and railing of earlier children's writers, and by the middle of the century far more liberal views were beginning to come into fashion. For the first time parents realised that their children had a right to enjoy themselves, and indeed that it might be good for them to do so; and with this realisation came—at least from the upper classes—a new demand for toys.

Although juvenile literature is a huge subject quite outside the scope of this book, it is inextricably bound up with the development of toys, and the publication of *A Little Pretty Pocket Book* in 1744 highlights the new trend most conveniently. *A Little Pretty Pocket Book* was the first children's book aimed to *amuse* rather than only to instruct, and it was a runaway success. The far-sighted publisher was John Newbery, who followed it with many similar titles as well as with ingenious board games designed to entertain the young players while at the same time gently educating or improving them. Incidentally, it is interesting to find that Newbery encouraged the sale of *A Little Pretty Pocket Book* (which cost sixpence) by throwing in a pincushion or a ball for an extra penny. This seems to be the earliest recorded 'premium offer', and it is significant that such a promotion scheme should have featured toys; since then many other playthings have been used to help retail sales, from Victorian wax dolls offered in exchange for tea coupons (see The Harris Museum, Preston) to small plastic figures secreted in corn flakes packets.

The change for the better was a gradual one, of course, but with the second half of the eighteenth century the whole attitude to childhood softened in a remarkable way. Quite a number of toys of this period have survived—particularly the characteristic wooden dolls with their dark glass eyes—and we know even more about them from contemporary portraits and diaries. Mrs. Delaney, Horace Walpole and Parson Woodforde all refer to toys—miniature tea sets, dolls, tops and—in Parson Woodforde's case—a paper caravan costing one and sixpence. By a stroke of luck a collection of bills for playthings bought by Viscount Irwin for his five little daughters at Temple Newsam was preserved with the household accounts covering the years 1762/68. Lord and Lady Irwin seem to have been very indulgent parents, and their purchases included willow rattles, 'glass ey'd Babies', a coach and two horses in a box, three sets of toy mops and brushes, a lady in a boat, a dozen plates (for sixpence) and a toy bureau which was evidently a craftsman-made piece, for it cost six shillings. Reynolds, Zoffany, Morland and William Hamilton are among the artists of this time who painted English children with wooden dolls, model ships, pull-along horses and other toys far more spectacular than anything that had gone before. At the same time children's clothes became much simpler, with trousers instead of breeches for little boys and plain dresses with wide sashes for girls. (A short-lived reprieve, as it happened: children were soon put back into very complicated garments, even when playing at the seaside; and Queen Victoria seized every opportunity to plunge her entire family, infants included, into the deepest mourning.)

This new consideration for children would in itself have been enough to have stimulated the toy trade, but equally important were the completely new production techniques which revolutionised the whole industry at about the same time. Until now virtually all toys, except for a few costly articles made specially by silversmiths and clockmakers, had been made of wood or earthenware, and largely by hand. But now everything began to surge forward, as new methods were applied to new materials: paper was used more and more, and most successfully, for beautifully-engraved cut-out toys; more important still, mass-produced metal toys came on to the market for the first time.

Metal figures

The most celebrated of these new models were made by the Hilpert family of Nuremberg. Inspired by the military exploits of Frederick the Great, they produced whole armies of small tin soldiers which they cast in shallow engraved moulds. 'Old Fritz' himself—an imposing equestrian figure— was one of the first to appear, in about 1775. As well as soldiers, the Hilperts made charming rococo gardens with hedges and fountains and elegant groups of people, and collections of animals based very accurately on detailed drawings (plate 2). Sometimes the animal's Latin name was engraved on the stand, to give the toy an extra educational value.

Other German firms were soon competing with the Hilperts in the production of these flat metal figures, including Heinrichsen of Nuremberg and Allgeyer of Furth. The most important thing about toy soldiers has always been to have plenty of them—they are far more effective in large numbers no matter whether made of paper, wood or tin—and the fact that they could now be mass-produced so easily was a great advantage. It was desirable, too, to avoid the absurdity of giants fighting battles with dwarfs, and by the 1840s agreement had been reached between the chief manufacturers on a uniform scale—known as the Nuremberg scale—which meant that a grown man should be about 30 mm. high.

Paper toys

The paper toys of the eighteenth century were within the means of comparatively poor families, since they could be bought as flat engraved sheets, and cut out and made up at home. Stiff paper soldiers were being played with years before Hilpert introduced his tin warriors, and there were also paper rooms with cut-out figures to be stuck on to them—a two-dimensional dolls' house, in fact. Paper dolls with an assortment of detachable clothes were certainly in existence before the end of the eighteenth century, and seem to have been an English invention: at any rate, they were always known as 'English dolls', even in Germany.

Peep-show pictures, which pulled out concertina-fashion, consisted of some spectacular view cut out in several planes

Nineteenth century German wooden toy.

which were then arranged one behind the other in proper perspective. Scenes showing fireworks and illuminations, or long vistas with baroque fountains, were popular eighteenth century choices; later toy peepshows were sold as souvenirs at the opening of the Thames Tunnel and at the Great Exhibition of 1851. Perhaps it is a sad comment on twentieth century architecture that this delightful toy has not been revived more often, although a new version was produced for the Silver Jubilee in 1977.

There were several toyshops in London by the 1760s, mostly to be found in the Holborn area. The original Hamley's, called The Noah's Ark, was at No. 231 High Holborn, and nearby was The Green Parrot, advertising 'Fine Babies and Baby-Houses, with all Sorts of Furniture at the lowest Price'. To the contemporary shopper, however, the word toy included a wide variety of small trinkets—watch chains, snuff boxes, scent bottles and the like—as well as children's playthings, and these shops did not by any means cater exclusively for the nursery.

Dolls' houses

Besides shop-bought toys, there were wonderful models made by the carpenters employed on great English country estates—dolls' houses, miniature furniture and scaled-down replicas of carriages and farm waggons of this period have all been preserved. The dolls' houses, or baby-houses to give them their usual eighteenth century name, were particularly impressive, and many of them can still be seen. These models had originated in Germany and the Netherlands not as toys but as cabinets for the display of valuable miniature objects, often made of silver, but English baby-houses always seem to have been much more toy-like than these early continental examples. One of the oldest to have survived was certainly intended for a child: it was a gift from Queen Anne to her god-daughter Ann Sharp at the very beginning of the eighteenth century. This remarkable house still has its original dolls, with the labels pinned to them by Ann Sharp giving their names—Fanny Long, ye Chambermaid, Roger ye Butler, Mrs. Hannah ye Housekeeper and several others of higher social standing. The house is very fully equipped, right down to a *baby-house* baby-house with its own furniture, all made of paper.

Another exceptional house is at Nostell Priory, near Wakefield in Yorkshire, built by the estate carpenter in about 1740. James Paine was the architect then working on Nostell Priory itself, and the baby-house broadly follows the same style with its Ionic columns and pediment. This is a toy of such magnificence that it can never have been played with except under the strictest supervision—indeed it was evidently intended originally to amuse the ladies of the house; its marble chimney pieces, exquisite fenders, wallpapers, bed-hangings—even the tinder box—are still like new after more than two hundred years. Many other really wonderful baby-houses of this vintage period are on view in museums and houses open to the public, notably the elaborate example at Uppark in Sussex, the Tate Baby-house in the Bethnal Green Museum, and Mrs. Graham Greene's unique collection of houses at The Rotunda, in Oxford.

Jig-saw puzzles

As well as these complete mansions, single open-fronted rooms were made, usually representing kitchens. Filled with batteries of miniature pots and pans and all sorts of domestic equipment, they were aimed at teaching little girls about housekeeping, and in this sense they were educational toys. Another eighteenth century plaything which set out to instruct as well as to amuse was the jig-saw puzzle—or dissected puzzle as it was then called, the jig not being invented until a century later. These puzzles, along with the growing number of children's books and table games, were mostly produced by the printers and map makers trading near St. Paul's Cathedral, London. Dissected maps, from which of course the child was intended to absorb geography fairly painlessly, were certainly in existence in the early 1760s. One small boy of four years old, according to the poet William Cowper, knew 'the situation of every kingdom, country, city, river and remarkable mountain in the world' thanks to 'those maps which are cut into several compartments, so as to be thrown into a heap of confusion that they may be put together again . . . to form a perfect whole'. History too could be learned from dissected puzzles, and so could moral precepts. One published in 1789 was labelled 'For the instruction of Youth . . . to impress upon their minds a love to virtue and a hatred to vice', and had for its picture a tree with the fruits of evil—stealing, lying and gaming—hanging on bare branches, while the fruits of goodness—bravery, sobriety and so forth—burgeoned on other branches of great luxuriance. Made of mahogany and packed in stout mahogany boxes, these puzzles were certainly not cheap: they cost anything between seven and twelve shillings—more than many people earned in a week—and like so many other playthings were still only for the leisured classes.

11

Prison models

Even the French Revolution made a macabre contribution to the world of toys, for it produced a miniature guillotine which really worked. Guillotines and similar working models were made in England by French prisoners taken during the Napoleonic Wars, who whiled away years of captivity constructing what they could from meat bones, scraps of wood and the other bits and pieces lying about the prisons, and earned a little money by selling their creations to local residents. There were seven thousand prisoners at Norman Cross, near Peterborough, many of them skilled craftsmen who turned out detailed ship models, miniature buildings, automated ranks of marching soldiers and all sorts of board and table games. Many of these were toys for adults rather than children, but the marquetry Noah's arks, decorated with straw plucked from the prisoners' mattresses and filled with carved wooden animals, must have had pride of place in dozens of Regency nurseries.

Rather surprisingly, the gentle Goëthe would have liked a toy guillotine for his son August, and he wrote to his mother in Strasbourg asking her to buy one for him. August's grandmother refused, and wrote Goëthe a very forceful letter giving her reasons. A less controversial present was the miniature theatre which August was given for one of his birthdays, and for which Goëthe painted some of the scenery; the toy theatre was very popular in the early nineteenth century, and condensed versions of contemporary dramas were specially written for nursery performances.

Nineteenth century toys

New toys now appeared on the English market in a steady stream, huge quantities being imported from Germany. Illustrated catalogues were already being issued by Nuremberg wholesalers before 1800, and these documents take a lot of the guesswork out of dating toys. Over 1,200 different items are listed in one of the earliest known catalogues—Bestelmeier's—including flat tin soldiers, balancing and mechanical figures, houses and formal gardens to be arranged on a table, tiny carriages and air balloons and page after page of other toys. Nelson's little daughter Horatia was painted holding a doll, and a boat, a carriage and one or two of her other playthings are on display at the National Maritime Museum, Greenwich. Small toys were much in demand at Christmas time for decorating the tree: John Watkins, in his *Memoirs of Queen Charlotte* published in 1819, describes a

Christmas party at Windsor with 'an immense tub with a yew-tree placed in it, from the branches of which hung bunches of sweet-meats, almonds and raisins, in papers, fruits, and toys, most tastefully arranged, and the whole illuminated by small wax candles . . . each child obtained a portion of the sweets which it bore, together with a toy, and then all returned home quite delighted'. So much, apparently, for the tradition that Prince Albert brought the Christmas tree to England.

Several toys that Queen Victoria had as a child are at Kensington Palace and the Museum of London including the 'Dutch' dolls she and her governess dressed with such care, a musical box with mechanical dancing figures, and a rather austere two-roomed dolls' house; if these are anything to go by, poor little Victoria does not seem to have fared so well as many of her future subjects.

A Biberach catalogue of about 1836 in the Bethnal Green Museum shows that the range of toys then offered was wider than ever: mounted stags' heads for the dolls' house hall were just one example of the German toymakers' ingenuity. The famous wooden soldiers which so delighted the young Brontë children, and which inspired their astonishing fantasies about the imaginary land of Angria, also belong to this period. Besides these invaluable trade catalogues, other useful sources of information are the Patent Office Registers and—from 1842 onwards—the Design Registers now kept at the Public Record Office's Repository at Ashridge. It comes as something of a surprise, for instance, to find that the kaleidoscope was patented by Sir David Brewster as early as 1817.

Optical toys

Kaleidoscopes are still popular toys today, and a very sophisticated version has been developed which dispenses with the old fragments of coloured glass and instead turns no matter what object viewed through it into an elegant pattern of reflections. But in 1817 a child would have been expected to know how these geometrical patterns were formed, for a toy of this kind also had an educational purpose. Other optical toys were soon to follow, based on the phenomenon of the persistence of vision: the idea behind them was a very simple one, often demonstrated by a child waving a sparkler round in an apparently unbroken circle of light on Guy Fawkes' Night. Introduced in 1826, the thaumatrope was the first of these 'persistence of vision' toys, consisting of a cardboard disc with a related drawing on each side—a parrot and a cage, perhaps, or a horse and jockey. The disc was rotated by means of threads attached to opposite points of the circumference, and the eye saw both images together—hence the parrot appeared to be in the cage, and the rider on the horse. The first *moving* picture illusion was produced by the phenakistoscope (also called the stroboscope and fantascope), which worked by presenting the eye with a rapid succession of figures in slightly different positions. The figures were drawn on a cardboard 'wheel', which had to be revolved very fast in front of a mirror; the reflected pictures were viewed through slots cut round the edge of the disc, and appeared to be moving.

The zoetrope, which was introduced about 1860, and the praxinoscope (patented in 1877) were improvements based on the same idea as the phenakistoscope, and the way this idea led eventually to the true moving picture film is clearly demonstrated by a series of exhibits in the Science Museum at South Kensington.

Many other toys are listed in the Patent Office Registers of the nineteenth century. In 1823 came what sounds like the invention of roller skates—'a machine to be attached to boots, shoes or other covering for the feet, for the purposes of travelling or pleasure'. A discovery which must have been warmly welcomed concerned 'Improvements to Pharoah's serpent'—the great improvement being that this popular indoor firework no longer smelled so strongly of sulpho-cyanide of mercury. India rubber and gutta-percha were new materials featured in patents of the 1850s, and there are detailed specifications of complicated mechanisms for making toy horses gallop, and dolls walk. The best-known walking doll was probably the Autoperipatetikos, which first appeared in America in 1862 (plate 9); an English patent was taken out in the same year. These dolls must have been fitted with exceptionally strong clockwork, for a great many of them, with their high-stepping metal feet, are still in perfect working order and can be seen in several museum collections.

The survival rate

A tremendous number of toys have survived from the middle years of the nineteenth century. Labour was still cheap enough for many of them to be finished by hand, and as yet there was little sign of the over-elaboration and poor design which characterised certain later playthings—some dolls' houses of the 1880s and 1890s are obvious examples. But the mid-century Noah's arks, the Montanari wax dolls, the miniature butchers' shops and early japanned tinplate trains (plate 5) were altogether delightful by any standard and, luckily for us, many of them were evidently very carefully looked after. Indeed, from the abundance still to be found today, not only in museums but also in superb private collections, antique shops and famous auction rooms, it might be imagined that there were no casualties at all; but the breakage rate for china dolls must have been very high, and wax dolls were even more vulnerable; many of them must have come to a sad end in the sun, and one wonders what happened to the flaxen-haired beauties which went with their young owners to India. Even though Noah's arks, because of their Old Testament connection, were often kept as 'Sunday toys' and so escaped some of the rough-and-tumble of nursery life, their animal inmates were notoriously brittle and before long there would be a sediment of broken legs, ears and tails lying in the bottom of the hull. Added to these natural disasters, boys in Victorian days could be as destructive as ever they were, and a particularly horrifying illustration by A. B. Houghton (fully as sinister as anything conceived by Gustave Doré) shows a boy beheading his sister's doll with a carpentry set. Jean Inglelow wrote a poem called *Law and Justice* to go with the drawing, typifying—according to the Dalziel Brothers who published it in one of their lavish gift books—'the children's little world of cloud and sunshine'

> *Now, this is Mary Queen of Scots!*
> *Push all her curls away;*
> *For we have heard about her plots,*
> *And she must die to-day.*

> *What's this? I must not hurt her so;*
> *You love her dearly still;*
> *You think she will be good—Oh no!*
> *I say she never will.*

> *My own new saw, and made of steel!*
> *Oh silly child to cry;*
> *She's only wood; she cannot feel;*
> *And, look, her eyes are dry.*

> *Her cheeks are bright with rosy spots;*
> *I know she cares for none—*
> *Besides, she's Mary Queen of Scots,*
> *And so it MUST be done.*

Toy shops and street sellers

But if some toys were destroyed there was no shortage of replacements. In London great toy emporiums like the Lowther Arcade, the Soho Bazaar and Cremer's of Regent Street literally overflowed with every sort of delight. One curmudgeon complained bitterly about the shopkeepers who blocked the passageways of the Lowther Arcade (which lay to the north side of the Strand near Charing Cross) with drums, children's tea things, 'Birmingham and Wedgwood trumperies', rocking horses and lambswool poodles. Besides these there were model theatres, magic lanterns, dolls of all sorts and sizes, clockwork trains, musical automata, dolls' houses with every imaginable piece of furniture, three-wheeled prams, balancing figures, miniature shops, building bricks and castellated forts—the vast plenty of the mid-nineteenth century toyshop defies being catalogued: no mere stock-list can compete with *The Cricket on the Hearth* and Dickens's picture of Tackleton the Toy Merchant with his 'hideous, hairy, red-eyed Jacks-in-Boxes . . . brown-paper farmers who drove pigs to market . . . movable old ladies who darned stockings or carved pies . . . and demoniacal Tumblers who wouldn't lie down, and were perpetually flying forward, to stare infants out of countenance'. A few pages further on, Caleb Plummer and his blind daughter are sitting in their workroom surrounded by 'houses for Dolls of all stations in life . . . scores of melancholy little carts which, when the wheels went round, performed most doleful music. Many small fiddles, drums and other instruments of torture; no end of cannon, shields, swords, spears and guns. There were little tumblers in red breeches, incessantly swarming up high obstacles of red-tape, and coming down, head first, on the other side; and there were innumerable old gentlemen of respectable, not to say venerable, appearance, insanely flying over horizontal pegs, inserted for the purpose in their own street doors. There were beasts of all sorts, horses in particular, of every breed, from the spotted barrel on four pegs, with a small tippet for a mane, to the thoroughbred rocker on his highest mettle'. Descriptions like this are interesting for the light they throw on the ordinary, everyday playthings of the new middle class; by and large it is the rather more expensive toys which have survived in museum collections, as naturally these were treated more carefully. But *The Cricket on the Hearth* has immortalised the expendable playthings of a generation of children 'who had played with them, and found them out, and broken them, and gone to sleep'. The original illustrations by John Leech are equally valuable, for his drawings of Caleb Plummer's workroom and all the toys are marvellously detailed.

Unpretentious little trifles were still sold by street vendors, and contemporary accounts of the famous 'Cries of London' include the 'Troop every one' of the hobby-horse seller,

'Young lambs to sell' and 'Buy a doll, Miss'. Later, towards the end of the nineteenth century and the beginning of the twentieth, hundreds of 'penny toys' could be bought from the hawkers on Ludgate Hill, and a collection of 1,600—all different and mostly made in Germany—was presented to the London Museum by Mr. Ernest King. Even today toys are much in evidence on London pavements, especially at Christmas time, and Dickens would have felt quite at home with the furry black spiders and clockwork crawling babies which emerge from giant suitcases and still enliven the kerbside until a policeman moves them on.

Victorian toyshops were still stocked largely with goods imported from Germany, where the guild system had finally been replaced with the latest industrial methods and up-to-date factories. English makers, though, were famous for sturdy wooden toys like wheelbarrows, carts, tool chests and dolls' houses, as well as wax dolls, humming tops, board games and educational toys, mechanical figures and miniature tea and dinner services.

Pottery toys

These pottery toys—mostly from Staffordshire—were particularly charming, and were turned out by the thousand. Even in the eighteenth century miniature pieces of china had been made for baby-houses—there is a set of delicate pierced Leeds ware in Ann Sharp's house—but as soon as transfer-printing on earthware became a practical proposition mugs and plates cheap enough for children's own use had been produced. At first the decorations had tended to be improving or educational, with moral verses, Biblical scenes or at best pictures of little girls giving refreshment to beggars, but as

Nineteenth century French dolls' pram.

17

the nineteenth century wore on the transfers got far gayer, and besides child-size pieces the potteries began to make tea and dinner services for dolls. Huge numbers are still to be found, complete with tureens, sauce-boats, ladles and sets of a dozen assorted plates, all printed with fairy story characters or other little scenes suitable for the nursery. Perhaps this is the moment to spare a thought for the multitude of forgotten children who suffered rather than benefited from the industrial revolution: many of them, often only eight years old, were employed in the potteries as well as in the mills and mines, and an official report published in 1842 mentions a boy of nine called William Cotton who worked in Longton for seventy hours a week, earning two shillings for making nearly three thousand earthenware figures. Whole families, children included, used to combine to colour book illustrations, or to make up dolls which other children then played with. Things gradually improved, thanks to social reformers like Lord Shaftesbury and to more enlightened legislation, but there were many real-life children whose lives were fully as terrible as Tom's in *The Water Babies.* Even Flora Thompson, who writes so movingly of her comparatively happy childhood in *Lark Rise to Candleford,* hardly mentions toys, and as a working-class child living deep in the country in the 1880s she probably saw very few. For her, the May Day doll, kept in the school needlework box and brought out only once a year for the traditional procession round the village, was still a thing of wonder.

Changes in fashion and technique

But most children whose families could afford to indulge them had nurseries full of toys. Towards the end of the nineteenth century there were even more mass-produced metal goods—tinplate ships and trains, filigree dolls' house furniture and clockwork figures—and novelties like stone building blocks and incredibly elaborate French dolls. Jumeau and Bru were the most famous Parisian doll-making firms, and one quickly comes to recognise their dolls by their expressive faces and—particularly in the case of the Jumeaus—their huge, rather owl-like, eyes. Often whole trunk-loads of clothes and accessories were supplied with them, so that they could be dressed in all the latest fashions. Other expensive dolls of this period could walk, talk and swim, and there were others with two or three faces so that they could be made to sleep, smile or cry by turning a knob on top of the head. One three-faced doll which must have alarmed many a sensitive child combined the characters of Red Riding Hood, the Grandmother and worst of all the Wolf—surely a psychiatrist's nightmare.

Not all parents approved of such elaborate playthings, and then as now there was much heart-searching among intellectuals as to what constituted a good and healthy toy. Ellen Terry, for example, would only let her children have things made of wood, and if a friend was unwise enough to give them anything which she considered unsuitable it was immediately taken away and burned. A clockwork mouse suffered this fate, condemned as 'realistic and common'. The darling of these aesthetic families was Walter Crane; besides producing children's books revolutionary in their simplicity, he designed nursery wallpapers with fairy-story characters woven into sinuous patterns of pale greens, blues and yellows which were eagerly snapped up by mothers with pre-Raphaelite tendencies. Some of the drawings of Randolph Caldecott, too, were adapted for rather brighter nursery wallpapers, and Kate Greenaway's delightful little vignettes were used for yet another paper of great charm which was still in production in the 1920s.

Advances in printing techniques played a great part in the development of toys in the second half of the nineteenth century. Rag books designed to stand up to hard wear and tear were a practical innovation, and it is interesting to find in the library of the Victoria and Albert Museum an edition of Watts's *Divine and Moral Songs* printed on linen in about 1850. The increased use of chromo-lithography meant that there were far more books with coloured illustrations, and it is sometimes difficult to know where to draw the line between toys and nursery books: there were books about animals, for instance, which also contained a bellows mechanism so that animal noises were emitted when the appropriate strings were pulled; bright 'pop-up' scenes sprang into life at the turn of a page, and other books for the very young were—and still are—shaped like animals and dolls. The Nuremberg firm of Ernest Nister was responsible for some particularly subtle colour printing, and one of their books had for its cover the facade of a dolls' house, complete with sloping roof and chimneys. The same delicate colours are found on picture blocks—sets of wooden cubes which can be rearranged to form six different pictures—and on German toy theatres. While the English juvenile drama remained faithful to the 'penny plain and twopence coloured' tradition of the old engraved sheets, Germany produced fanciful theatres which could be manipulated by quite small children, simply by turning a handle at the side of the stage, and winding new printed scenes into view.

Brilliant embossed paper scraps were another German speciality exported to England, angelic-looking children, puppies, kittens and flowers being the most usual subjects. Children stuck them into albums, and were sometimes allowed to help make a scrap screen for the nursery; considerable skill was called for in arranging portraits of the Royal Family and other coloured prints cut from magazines inside frames of scraps, and nothing evokes so clearly the atmosphere of those late Victorian nurseries with their nannies, brass fireguards and fumes from the Magic Lantern.

Edwardian toys

Edwardian toymakers were as enterprising as ever, and with the new century English firms began to rival their German counterparts. William Harbutt had invented Plasticine in 1897, and although he started in a very modest way and most of his sales were through small advertisements in various magazines, the educational possibilities of this new medium were soon realised and business quickly increased. One of the minor pleasures of discovering the playthings of this period is to find a toy still with its original box, as the lids are often charmingly decorated (plate 11): one of Harbutt's first outfits was called 'The Child's Delight' ('Plasticine is something new, and hopes to make a friend of you') and showed two children modelling a large elephant. Similar lids giving a somewhat exaggerated idea of the contents were used for boxes of building bricks—they usually implied that a towering edifice could be made from the smallest box—and a few years later nursery games were shown being played by laughing families in immaculate evening dress.

William Britain had first put his toy soldiers on the market in 1893, though long before this he and his family had specialised in producing high-quality clockwork figures—walking bears, coolies pulling rickshaws, and other ingenious automata. But these expensive models appealed only to a comparatively small market, and William Britain began to look further afield for ideas. So far as toy soldiers were concerned, the industry had always been dominated by Germany; by Britain's time solid, rounded soldiers were being produced in huge numbers and sold all over the world. Their disadvantage was that they were heavy and expensive, and with this in mind William Britain set about devising a new method of hollow-casting which made his figures cheaper and lighter than the German models. His sons did meticulous research into military history to make sure that every uniform was absolutely accurate, while the daughters, who had origin-

20

ally made clothes for the clockwork toys, did the painting. Gamages were renowned for their toy department, and when they began to stock Britain's soldiers the success of the new models was assured. As time went on farmyard animals, miniature gardens, boy scout encampments, cowboys, Indians and Zulu warriors were added to the range, as well as some dolls' house pieces which could be bought for a penny each. A push-chair, a coal scuttle and a tiny high chair are illustrated in a catalogue of about 1910, and these minuscule objects can still be seen in many old dolls' houses. Britains Ltd. continues, of course, to be a very successful toy-making concern, and although some reactionaries may deplore the switch to plastic soldiers there are no complaints from modern children.

Complete Clockwork Trains.

(IN CORRECT RAILWAY CO'S. COLOURS).

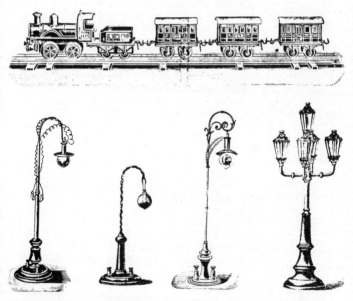

Two illustrations from Bassett-Lowke's early catalogues. The clockwork train appears in the 1903-4 edition, the miniature lamps in the 1904-5 edition.

Frank Hornby was another English toymaker whose name has become a household word. Besides being celebrated for clockwork and electric trains, he has gone down in history as the inventor of Meccano. In fact the idea for Meccano came to him first while he was watching a crane near the Liverpool office where he worked. In 1901 he took out a patent for a constructional toy made up of perforated metal parts, but it was some years before he could persuade a manufacturer that Mechanics Made Easy—the original name—was a commercial proposition. After the First World War the Meccano Company expanded first into the clockwork train market, and then into electric trains.

Dinky toys, most famous of all diecast metal cars, were originally intended as accessories for Hornby model railway lay-outs, and were made by Meccano Ltd. Introduced in 1934, they were made principally of lead with realistic tinplate radiators, and were tremendously popular until the Second World War put a stop to the production of metal toys. About the middle of 1946 new models of cars and aeroplanes were released, but Dinky toys had to face growing competition from Corgi and Lesney, and in 1964 the company was taken over by Lines Brothers.

Returning to Edwardian toys, the first known Bassett-Lowke catalogue appeared in 1901, and for the next thirty years or more it was every boy's ambition to own one of the superb model steam locomotives manufactured by this firm. Many readers will remember their shop at 112 High Holborn where engineering marvels like the model of Stephenson's Rocket with 'strong brass boiler, patent spirit lamp, double-action slide valve cylinders, whistle and safety valve' and locomotives of the famous Black Prince series could be bought. Besides the locomotives produced at his Northampton factory, W. J. Bassett-Lowke arranged for various German firms to supply him with models specially adapted for the British market: the well-known Bing Table Railways were one result of this association. Although the shop in High Holborn has disappeared, the model railway connoisseur can still visit 'The Steam Age' in Cadogan Street, London, S.W.3. and admire selected new and second-hand engines and rolling stock; but these marvels now lie within the province of adult toys.

The gollywogg

The English writer Florence Upton was alone responsible for the gollywogg. In 1895 Warne published her book *The Adventures of Two Dutch Dolls and a Golliwogg*, which she based on a black doll which had been brought over from the United States when her grandmother was a child. According to John Leech's drawings, a similar sort of grotesque black doll was usually the one chosen for the early Jack-in-a-Box toy, but whatever its basic origin the new turn-of-the-century gollywogg made an immediate impact and still survives virtually unchanged.

The teddy bear

Significant as these British successes were, however, it must be admitted that the most popular newcomer of all—the teddy bear—was not one of our inventions. The bear cub which unwittingly inspired a whole new industry was American: President Theodore Roosevelt had come upon the little animal in 1902 while on a hunting trip in Mississippi, and a political cartoonist had made a drawing of the President refusing to shoot it. The first toy bear based on the drawing seems to have been made by an American called Morris Michtom, who obtained the President's permission for the bear to be named after him. At about the same time a talented German toymaker, Margaret Steiff, was working on various soft animal toys, including bears, and some experts claim that *her* bear was first in the field. At all events, the Steiff company was soon exporting many thousands of teddy bears every year, and there has never been any doubt about the toy's success. Over the years there have been minor changes—the nose has become less classical, the fur washable, and the old rumbling growl has given way to a squeak—but the teddy bear has remained a universal favourite, beloved alike by boys and girls.

Samuel Finburgh & Co., an English firm, produced a cut-out sheet for making up into a flannelette teddy bear in 1909. This sort of fabric cut-out sheet was very popular, and similar ones were issued by Dean's Rag Book Co. Ltd. Besides conventional child dolls, characters like gollywoggs, First World War Tommies and Struwwelpeters could be made up very cheaply by this method, and the idea has recently been revived. 'Myfanwy Jones', a cut-out doll designed by Margaret Holgate, was outstanding amongst the souvenirs of the Investiture of the Prince of Wales in 1969.

The magic lantern

Alongside all the innovations of the early twentieth century, with its new ideas and streamlined production techniques, many old favourites managed to hold their own. The Army and Navy Stores catalogue for 1907, recently reprinted under the title *Yesterday's Shopping,* shows that magic lanterns were still much in demand: they had in fact been known in England since the 1660s, and in his *Diary* Pepys describes a demonstration in 1665. Slides—educational and otherwise—suitable for nursery viewing were produced all through the nineteenth century, and in 1907 a wide assortment including 'The Three Bears', 'The House that Jack Built' and 'Our Lifeboatman' was still competing with the novelty of the cinema. Also listed, under Compendiums of Games, were Pope Joan and Fox and Geese, which one might think would have been thoroughly obsolete by this time. Most of the toys were still very Victorian-looking—no doubt 'The Stores' tended to be conservative—and the woodcut illustrations include curvaceous wicker perambulators, sturdy metal cooking stoves, wooden carts and caravans and a horse tricycle exactly like the one Ernest Shepard had when he was a small boy in the 1880s, and which he recalls with such pleasure in his autobiography *Drawn from Memory.*

Other well-tried playthings were adapted to suit an ever-growing market where low prices were of paramount importance. In 1910 a Nuremberg firm was able to offer a collapsible cardboard Noah's ark with 24 animals at 8/8d. per *dozen,* wholesale. Cardboard was used too for Jolly Jumpers, amusing little jointed figures derived from the Victorian jumping jack and even earlier French *pantin,* and for shops and post offices which were directly descended from the old Nuremberg kitchens. Catalogues of this period also show a trend towards more 'occupational' toys—sets of blacksmith's tools, potter's wheels and conjuring outfits were recommended as Christmas presents for boys, while girls were given embroidery and basket-making kits. All sorts of card and board games were good selling lines, including many variations on the old game of picture lotto (later, incidentally, to undergo the strangest metamorphosis and to emerge as bingo).

Toys of the inter-war years

The toy industry made an amazingly quick recovery after the 1914-1918 war, and British firms went from strength to strength. So far as china dolls were concerned, though, German manufacturers still had a monopoly; besides supplying new dolls they did a roaring trade in replacement heads which were fitted at the dolls' hospitals that used to play such an important part in a child's life. In spite of being dangerously inflammable, celluloid dolls and animals were very popular in the 1920s and 1930s: there were tiny boats which, powered only by a crumb of camphor, sped magically across a bowl of water, and brightly-coloured fish and ducks for floating in the bath. They were very fragile, and soon got dented; sometimes the dent could be sucked out, or the toy could be gently prised back into shape with a pin, but if these remedies failed it could easily be replaced for a penny or two. The turnover must have been immense.

SPEAR'S JOLLY JUMPERS.

THE great success of the 3 designs brought out last year (see supplement 6), has induced us to bring out a few more patterns, which are illustrated below. Spear's Jolly Jumpers are finished in bright colors, are very solidly made and are rivetted at the joints, and we can recommend this line as a most durable toy.

| DUTCHMAN. | RED INDIAN. | HUMPTY DUMPTY. | GALLOPING MAJOR. |

No. 5753. Price 4/8 per dozen. No. 5782. Price 4/8 per dozen. No. 5666. Price 4/8 per dozen. No. 5700. Price 4/8 per dozen.

"SNOWBALL." "FIDO."

"SNOWBALL."
No. 5782.
Price 4/8 per dozen.

"FIDO."
No. 5781.
Price 4/8 per dozen.

TWO NEW LINES OF DISSECTED PUZZLES.

EACH box containing 4 layers of cut-up Puzzles, wrapped in transparent paper, so that no pieces can be lost. For other styles of Dissected Puzzles, see supplements No. 4, 5 and 6.

| FARM and DAIRY. | SOLDIERS of the EMPIRE. |

No. 5721/2 ... price 8/8 per dozen. No. 5689/2 ... price 8/8 per dozen.

(7)

A page from a Nuremberg trade catalogue c. 1910. (Courtesy of J. W. Spear & Sons Ltd.)

Mascot toys

All kinds of mascot toys were produced in the inter-war period, and the one which people seem to remember best is Sunny Jim (plate 21). This odd-looking rag doll originated in the United States and made its first appearance in England in the early 1920s; it was (and in fact still is) given in exchange for coupons collected from Force cereal packets. Firms like Chad Valley, Norah Wellings and Merrythought made other soft toys based on newspaper or film characters, including Pip, Squeak and Wilfred, The Nipper (a Daily Mail cartoon child), Mickey Mouse and Snow White and the Seven Dwarfs. Nowadays of course we have toys inspired by television—The Wombles, Basil Brush and so on.

Monopoly

The depression of the 1930s probably had something to do with the fantastic popularity of Monopoly, for here was a game which could give people the illusion, at least, of having money to spend and speculate with. Appropriately enough, it was invented by an American, Mr. Charles B. Darrow, when he was out of work and finding it difficult to make ends meet. The original game he produced was most primitive—the board was hand drawn on a circular piece of linoleum and coloured with samples of paint; the title deed cards were typewritten on cardboard, and the houses and hotels cut from lengths of beading picked up at a local lumber yard. The game had been intended only for family amusement, but so many of Mr. Darrow's friends wanted a set that he made a few copies which he sold for four dollars each. He could only manage one or two sets a day, and demand quickly outstripped supply. Mr. Darrow then approached Parker Brothers, one of the biggest games manufacturers in the States, but they turned the idea down saying that it was too complicated to have any great appeal. However, like Frank Hornby, Charles Darrow persisted; when enquiries from retailers reached 20,000 a year he went back to Parker Brothers, who reconsidered their decision, and Monopoly was finally placed on the market in 1935. In England, a director of John Waddington Ltd. heard of the game, and arrangements were made for his firm to become the British licensee; although Waddingtons' playing card and games division now publishes a great many lines, Monopoly is still the best seller.

Wartime toys

With the outbreak of the Second World War the European toy trade came virtually to a standstill. Most British factories switched to making munitions, and only a few home-produced toys filtered through to the shops. Hamleys' advertisements in the weeks before Christmas 1939 show how quickly the market was affected: a wooden slide was recommended 'for the evacuated children', and bicycles 'for getting about in wartime'. A model Hurricane fighter cost 2/11d., and there were some rather aggressive-sounding games, like 'the exciting new A.R.P. game'—played with dice—which promised 'all the thrill of aeroplanes and air raids—try your skill shooting down planes'. But apart from a few toys like these, children had to make do with playthings handed down by older brothers and sisters, which is probably one of the reasons why toys of the 'thirties are comparatively difficult to find now, this double life-span being too much for most of them. There was a boom in knitting patterns for stuffed toys, mostly animals, which mothers could make at home, though even these had to be contrived from odds and ends as knitting wool was soon rationed. After the end of the war there was still an acute shortage of most of the raw materials needed for toy-making, and it was not until the late 1940s that the trade really began to recover.

Post-war developments

But with this gradual recovery came changes every bit as revolutionary as those which had transformed the world of toys in the mid-eighteenth century. For one thing there was a vast market ready and waiting, since parents wanted to indulge their children again, and make up for years of austerity and deprivation; in the new welfare state people felt they had money to spend on luxuries, and pocket-money climbed to heights undreamed of in the 'thirties. More important still, new plastic materials had a profound effect on the industry, completely replacing china and celluloid for dolls and soon ousting metal and wood in the manufacture of many other toys. Besides being cheap, plastic was hygienic, unbreakable and non-toxic—everything, in fact, most desirable in the eyes of the new generation of mothers competing with each other on post-war housing estates. Some of these early toys were admittedly terrible, and it is easy enough to reject them all, as Ellen Terry did the clockwork mouse; but the fantastic detail which could be got into a small piece of moulded plastic was something which mass-production had never been able to achieve before, and manufacturers were quick to exploit its many possibilities. New materials may come and go, but the toys children have always wanted above all others are familiar, everyday objects reproduced in miniature, and thus given a magical extra dimension; the more realistic they are, the better. Most little girls today would rather have a talking doll made of vinyl, with hair that can be washed and set, than the loveliest Jumeau beauty; and a plastic secretaire five inches high, with drawers that open and slides to support the let-down flap, must rank in its way with the most coveted item in a Victorian dolls' house.

'Matchbox' models

Intense realism again accounts for much of the success of Lesney's 'Matchbox' toys. The firm was founded in 1947 when two young ex-service men, John Odell and Leslie Smith, pooled their gratuities and began making pressure die-castings for industry in an old pub in Tottenham. A steady business was built up, and in 1949 they produced a few diecast metal toys, more or less as a side-line, to keep some sections of their small factory fully operating. The forerunner of the 'Matchbox' models was a state processional coach with a team of horses, sixteen inches long altogether, which appeared in 1950. Few of these original coaches were made because the outbreak of the Korean War meant a ban on the use of zinc, but when Queen Elizabeth came to the throne in 1952 the directors realised that the same coach in miniature would make a perfect Coronation souvenir. This smaller coach was just over five inches long—including horses—and can be identified by the words 'Lesney England' printed on the under-carriage. It cost 2/11d., and well over a million models were sold.

An assortment of tiny vehicles packed in the now familiar imitation matchboxes came next, and the demand both at home and overseas was so great that Lesney were soon looking for bigger premises. 1955 saw the introduction of 'Models of Yesteryear', beautifully-made miniatures of vintage cars as popular with collectors and motoring enthusiasts as with children. By 1970 the output was running at some five and a half million 'Matchbox' models a week, with a large proportion being exported—a performance comparable with past achievements of German toy factories.

Action Man

Nearly all children enjoy building up a collection, whether of model cars, stamps or toy soldiers, and this is one of the reasons for the popularity of Action Man. This is a most unusual doll in that it appeals to boys, and once again it is intensely realistic. Action Man is an extrovert character, and can be supplied with all manner of different equipment, neatly packaged and sold separately, for such virile pursuits as fighting, space travel, polar exploration (complete with husky dogs), diving and mountaineering. His female counterpart is Sindy, a teenage doll with an extensive wardrobe, 'personalized' furniture, a sports car and a boy-friend called Paul. One can just recognise these figures as the mass-produced, many-times-removed descendants of the lavishly-costumed French dolls of the 1880s, all of them owing their attraction to the fact that they can be endlessly dressed and undressed.

New games

So far as games are concerned, the most popular to have appeared since the war is undoubtedly Scrabble, a grown-up variation on the old 'Word Making and Word Taking'. Invented by Mr. Butts, a New York architect, it was first produced in England in 1954 by Spear's Games, and has been selling steadily ever since. It is encouraging, though, to think that Spirograph, one of the most compulsive toys of recent years, is a completely British invention. It was the brainchild of an engineer, Mr. Denys Fisher, and grew out of his work on the operation of epicyclic gears. Technically, therefore, this is a very sophisticated toy, but its appeal has been proved in no uncertain terms and even quite small children can learn to handle the junior version, Spirotot.

Educational and traditional toys

Despite the importance of the mass-market and low prices, there are still specialist retailers who recognise the need for lasting, well-made playthings and cater for the trend towards greater simplicity; they supply strong climbing frames, plain building bricks, satisfying paint boxes and other constructional and creative toys designed to stimulate a child's imagination. It is interesting, incidentally, to compare these modern educational toys with those offered to children two centuries ago: then all the emphasis was on assimilating facts and learning moral values, while today it is considered thoroughly reprehensible to fill a child's mind with facts (witness the scorn heaped upon parents who tried to cram their offspring in preparation for the eleven-plus examination) and if toys set out to instruct at all then they must stick to manual dexterity and simple logic.

For many years psychologists and child guidance experts have used toys in assessing intelligence and diagnosing emotional troubles: a dolls' house is one of the most useful pieces of equipment in a London reception centre for disturbed children, and from the way a child plays with it and arranges the inmates a doctor can get valuable clues as to the sort of treatment needed. Cremer realised the importance of play a hundred years ago, when he wrote:

> 'A little golden-haired girl who had no doll of her own has grown up to be known amongst her friends as The Iceberg, and to be almost totally ignorant of sewing'.

Even allowing for his being a shopkeeper with a vested interest in selling dolls, and perhaps with an exaggerated regard for fine needlework, there is no doubt that he saw that play was essential to a child's emotional development. One of the most pathetic relics to have survived in any toy collection is the makeshift doll in the Museum of Childhood in Edinburgh, made years ago by a slum child out of an old shoe and a piece of rag.

Traditional folk toys still manage to compete with modern factory-made goods. The Russian Shop in Holborn, for instance, sells the well-known 'pecking chickens' weighted toy, and other simple wooden movement figures like bears riding tricycles or thumping grand pianos. Small dolls made from sweet-corn husks are still imported from Czechoslovakia, and oval wooden boxes, packed with turned soldiers or farmyard animals from Germany; from further afield there are brightly painted Indian beasts, silky Chinese birds, Japanese water flowers and kites, and tiny Mexican kitchen dressers.

Some of today's toys will undoubtedly become the antiques and museum pieces of to-morrow, and far-sighted investors may well be laying down examples in mint condition. After all, the Lesney Coronation Coach is a collectors' item already, and the miniature Dinky cars of the 1930s are certainly much sought after. Recently an entire London auction sale was devoted to lead soldiers—mostly William Britain's—and as for the best Victorian toys, the prices they fetch in the sale room are astronomical. French automata invariably go for several hundred pounds, and dolls' house furniture is often more expensive than full-sized pieces. Earlier toys and children's books are literally invaluable, and it is impossible to predict what will happen when an eighteenth century wooden doll or rocking horse comes on to the market.

But luckily for toy enthusiasts of modest resources, a great many lovely things are on display in various museums up and down the country, and the following list, while it is by no means exhaustive, will give some guidance to those wanting to find out more for themselves.

GAZETTEER OF MUSEUMS AND COLLECTIONS

The following museums all have collections of toys, but intending visitors, especially if travelling from a distance, should make a point of checking times of opening. Some of the smaller or more remote museums are closed altogether during the winter months.

It is also advisable to make sure that any particular item is in fact on display; most museums suffer from a chronic lack of space and may have only a selection of their toys on view at any one time. Arrangements can usually be made for *bona fide* collectors and serious students to see reserve collections by prior appointment.

AVON

Museum of Costume, Assembly Rooms, Bath
(tel: Bath 28803)
There is a fine display of dolls and, as might be expected, particularly good examples of dolls' clothing. Cut-out paper dolls for colouring and dressing are on sale (costume of 1830, 1860 or 1880)—a modern version of an English toy dating back to the late eighteenth century.

Burrows Toy Museum, The Octagon, 46 Milsom Street, Bath
(tel: Bath 4019)
One of the newest toy museums, this fascinating collection ranges from the products of prestige manufacturers to the humblest penny toy and covers the past century and a half. The exhibits of the 1920s and 1930s are especially interesting, for this was the age of the Promotional Toy—of Pip, Squeak and Wilfred and Felix the Cat. A visit is strongly recommended.

American Museum in Britain, Claverton Manor, Bath
(tel: Bath 60503)
Various early American toys are on show throughout the house, including a small rocking horse wearing a net to protect it from flies and a set of miniature rooms.

Blaise Castle House Museum, Henbury, Bristol
(tel: Bristol 625378)
A branch of Bristol City Museum, Blaise Castle has an extensive collection of nineteenth-century toys, with some

eighteenth-century dolls and early twentieth-century soldiers. Typical Victorian toys are arranged in a shop-window setting, and there are good examples of the more expensive large wooden toys—a pull-along train, miniature governess cart, rocking horse and some fine mahogany dolls' beds.

BEDFORDSHIRE

Bedford Museum, The Embankment, Bedford
(tel: Bedford 53323)

This old-style museum has a wonderfully varied assortment of exhibits, including a small collection of dolls and toys. Metal dolls' house furniture, magic lantern slides, a wax fairy doll in original clothes, a beautiful model greenhouse full of flowers and tiny 1930s dolls are particularly memorable.

Museum and Art Gallery, Wardown Park, Luton
(tel: Luton 36941)

The museum has many fine examples of commonplace early toys as well as more unusual items such as the dolls dressed by nineteenth-century straw-plait workers and a wax baby emerging from an Easter egg. There are dolls of the eighteenth, nineteenth and twentieth centuries, many varieties of optical toy, model engines, early twentieth-century clock-work cars, lead figures, dolls' house furniture, miniature pieces of porcelain and china, children's books, games, puzzles and jigsaws. Selected modern toys are also being collected.

BERKSHIRE

Windsor Castle

Visitors can see Queen Mary's famous dolls' house, designed by Sir Edwin Lutyens in the 1920s, and filled with specially made miniatures in perfect scale. Many of the country's finest craftsmen combined to make the furniture, all of it exquisite. The accessories range from leather dispatch boxes in the library to a knife-polishing machine in the kitchen, and the garage with its fleet of royal motorcars should be carefully noted. It was, of course, never intended as a toy to be played with, but rather as a cabinet for the display of valuable modern works of art. Older pieces of toy furniture, a selection of the small dolls dressed by Queen Victoria and dolls presented to members of the Royal Family in the course of their travels are shown near the dolls' house.

1. Wooden toy tiger with string-operated movable jaw, Egyptian, c. 1000 BC.

2. Moulded metal animals made in Nuremberg by the Hilpert family about 1780.

3. English dolls, late seventeenth century, known as 'Lord and Lady Clapham'. They have their original clothes, accessories and chairs.

4. Wooden rocking horse, English, early nineteenth century.

5. Clockwork tin train with original box, German, c. 1840.

6. Boat and sailor with clockwork mechanism in painted tin, wood and composition, English, 1869.

7. *A page from a Nuremberg wholesaler's catalogue, c. 1840.*

8. *Miniature books of juvenile instruction in decorative wooden cases, early nineteenth century.*

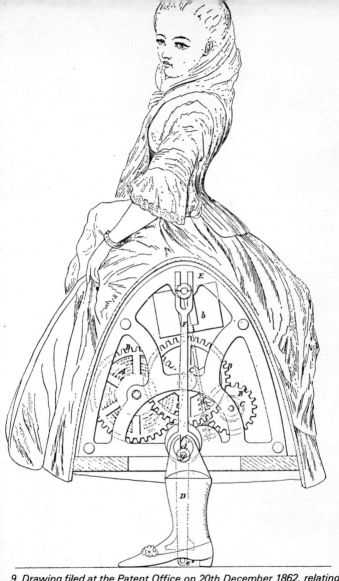

9. Drawing filed at the Patent Office on 20th December 1862, relating to 'Improvements in the Manufacture of Automatic Toy Figures'. Originating in America, this particular type of walking doll was known as the 'Autoperipatetikos'.

Because he is at Saddlebow

Why does this Man appear to

10. The two faces of a thaumatrope disc, c. 1826, a simple optical toy based on the persistence of vision.

11. The lid of a fantascope box, c. 1860. This toy, also known as the stroboscope and Phentakistoscope, was the first to produce a true moving picture illusion.

Living Pictures
Optical Illusion.

Tableaux vivants
Illusions optiques.

Lebende Bilder.

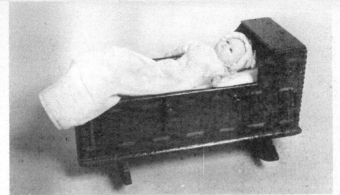

12. Composition German doll, c. 1850, in an eighteenth-century wooden cradle.

13. Child's transfer-printed plate with moulded border, English, c. 1840. The verse is from Isaac Watts's 'Divine and Moral Songs'.

The tulip and the butterfly.
Appear in gayer coats than I.

Let me be dress'd fine as I will,
Flies worms and flowers exceed me still.

14. The Rabbits' School, one of William Potter's group of stuffed animals, c. 1880-90.

15. 'The Picture Alphabet for a Good Child', hand-coloured cards in a wooden box, c. 1830.

16. A nineteenth-century brass locomotive.

17. This doll, only four inches high, and the miniature chair are typical of the high-quality dolls' house pieces produced in the second half of the nineteenth century.

ESKIMO DOLL,
in Plushette,
ces, 10½d., 1/4½, 1/11¾

The TINY TOTS' STORES,
contains real Sweets, Scales, &c.,
as illustrated.
Prices, 5¾d., 10¾d., 1/6½, 1/11¾

The PREMIER BOX of CON
TRICKS, containing a nu
of new and amusing tri
Prices, 5¾d., 10¾d., 1/6½

he POTTER'S WHEEL, with
odelling Clay, for spinning Cups
and Saucers, &c. Very
interesting, Price, 4/11

BLACKSMITH'S OUTFIT, fitted with Iron Tools,
as sketch. Price, 5/11

PLUSH TEDDY
the Children's favouri
10¾d., 1/6½, 1/11¾, 2/6

DOLL'S CHINA TEA SET,
well made and pretty designs,
vide as sketch.
Prices, 10¾d., 1/4½, 1/11¾

The Game of PARLOUR CROQUET,
for table play, Set of Balls, Mallets,
Hoops, &c.,
Prices, 9¾d., 1/3½
CARPET CROQUET, 4/11, 5/11

TINY TOT'S POST OFFIC
Stationery, Postal Stamps & D
Prices, 4¾d., 9¾d., 1/3½

HEELAS, SONS & CO LTD   BROAD STREET, READING

18. *Page from a Christmas catalogue issued by Heelas, Sons and Co.
Ltd, Reading, c. 1910.*

19. *Three of the 'Dolls in Wonderland' at Brighton. The two on the seesaw are French, the middle one is German. All belong to the last quarter of the nineteenth century.*

20. *Edwardian dolls photographed in the grounds of Penrhyn Castle. The dark-haired child doll is French, the other two are German.*

21. (Left) 'Sunny Jim' rag doll, advertising 'Force' wheat flakes.
22. 'Old Woman in Shoe', set of jointed dolls presented as a prize to a five-year-old schoolgirl in 1869.

23. Wooden soldiers on an extending base made in Germany for the British market, c. 1890.

24. Doll's house, Victorian, 1880. Wooden, covered with varnished brick paper.

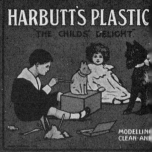

25. Lids from boxes of Harbutt's Plasticine, early twentieth century.

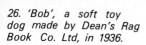

26. 'Bob', a soft toy dog made by Dean's Rag Book Co. Ltd, in 1936.

27. A late nineteenth-century high pram with reversible hood and decorative springing.

28. 'Snowbaby' Christmas-cake decorations of bisque porcelain, German, 1920-30.

29. Wax fairy doll, early twentieth century.

CAMBRIDGESHIRE

Cambridge and County Folk Museum, 2 & 3 Castle Street, Cambridge (tel: Cambridge 55159)

The early nursery equipment is especially interesting and includes eighteenth-century school text-books, baby-walkers, a castor-oil spoon and backboards for the prevention and cure of round shoulders. There is a rich variety of cots and cradles for both babies and dolls, an exceptionally large Noah's ark, dolls and other toys.

City Museum and Art Gallery, Priestgate, Peterborough (tel: Peterborough 3329)

French prisoners-of-war at nearby Norman Cross made many toys, games and working models, often more suitable for adults than for children, and the museum has a good collection of these. There is also an interesting Noah's ark made in the prison.

CORNWALL

Cornish Museum, Lower Street, East Looe (tel: Liskeard 2423)

This museum, illustrating the life and culture of Cornwall, has a section devoted to games and pastimes: it includes a set of Victorian Punch and Judy puppets in original costumes, lead farm animals and other toys, a collection of home-made dolls' hats and shoes dated from about 1815, and early children's books. There are also various perambulators, cribs and other pieces of nursery equipment.

Helston Borough Museum, Old Butter Market, Church Street, Helston

Traditionally boys always bowled iron hoops and girls wooden ones, and this museum has examples of both, as well as a skipping rope, marbles, tinware clockwork toys, a magic lantern and slides, a Victorian sand toy, dolls, books and other nursery bygones.

CUMBRIA

Hill Top, near Sawrey

This house is still very much as it was when Beatrix Potter lived here; there is a dolls' house with the original plates of plaster food featured in *The Tale of Two Bad Mice,* and some dolls wearing clothes she made specially for them when trying out designs for *The Tailor of Gloucester*.

DERBYSHIRE

Derbyshire County Museum, Sudbury Hall
'Exploring Childhood' is an exhibition about the life of children in the past which provides things for visitors, especially children, to do as well as see. There is a fine collection of early schoolbooks besides the more spectacular (and usual) Victorian dolls and nursery impedimenta. Do not miss the floor-level view through a mousehole.

DEVON

Royal Albert Memorial Museum and Art Gallery, Exeter (tel: Exeter 56724)
Although there are not enough toys on view to warrant a special trip, this collection should not be missed by any enthusiast who happens to be in the district. There are several eighteenth- and early nineteenth-century dolls and a number of attractive dolls' accessories including gloves, fans and parasols, a fur muff, an unusual chatelaine with pince-nez, scissors and crochet hook, and a crinoline frame with watch-spring stiffeners, c. 1862.

The Elizabethan House, 70 Fore Street, Totnes (tel: Totnes 863821)
A varied small collection of toys, mostly nineteenth-century, including about a dozen dolls and a fully furnished dolls' house. A good deal of Victorian dolls' house furniture was home-made, and this museum has a set made of feathers: there must have been quite a craze for this at one time and a surprising amount has survived. Goose quills were carefully trimmed, and then joined together in such a way that the feathery parts overlapped and formed quite convincing cane-seat chairs and other small items.

DORSET

Red House Museum and Art Gallery, Quay Road, Christchurch (tel: Christchurch 2860)
The local history room contains educational games and jigsaws (c. 1820), miniature kitchen equipment (c. 1870), a

collection of small clockwork toys, including a model of the Great Wheel at the Earls Court Exhibition, and numerous other games and toys. There is also a comprehensive display of about forty dolls, including one of the many parian portrait dolls made to represent Princess Alexandra at the time of her marriage to the then Prince of Wales in 1863.

Local History Museum, Gold Hill, Shaftesbury
(tel: Shaftesbury 2157)

A small museum, owned by the Shaftesbury and District Historical Society, contains a number of toys, Victorian by-gones and items of local interest.

DURHAM

North of England Open Air Museum, Beamish Hall, Stanley
(tel: Stanley 33580)

This is a new museum which opened in 1971. Dolls, Noah's arks, jigsaw puzzles, clockwork models and other Victorian and later toys are among the exhibits, as well as nursery equipment. The collections extend up to the present day.

Bowes Museum, Barnard Castle (tel: Barnard Castle 2139)

The toy collection includes a rare French 'Ondine' clockwork swimming doll, of the kind first patented in 1876. This is also the home of the famous mechanical silver swan (1740/50) made by the London clockmaker Richard Weekes; this remarkable bird, floating on a sparkling lake of twisting glass rods, lowers its head, catches a fish and eats it, all to a musical accompaniment. Although certainly not meant for children, it was from expensive clockwork models like this that the ingenious mechanical toys of the next century evolved.

EAST SUSSEX

Dolls in Wonderland, Seafront, Brighton
(tel: Brighton 27147)

Mrs Vera Kramer's exhibition of superb dolls appeals to both children and connoisseurs: while one group enjoys the fairy-tale tableaux, the other can appreciate the fine quality of the individual exhibits. Allow plenty of time, as there are many hundreds of items which will repay close examination. The detailed catalogue is especially useful.

Hove Museum of Art, 19 New Church Road, Hove
(tel: Brighton 779410)

Although quite small, the toy collection includes some attractive items: a little French bisque doll, c. 1880, with exquisite moulded hairstyle, and a large 1910 dolls' house with original friezes round the rooms, stick in the memory.

The Toy Museum, The Grange, Rottingdean
(tel: Brighton 31004)

This is a very large collection of toys, dolls and games from all over the world and includes some present-day examples. The exhibits are conveniently grouped in various sections—optical toys, the theatre, street play and so on. Especially interesting are the tools and materials used in making wax dolls, given by the late Mr J. C. Pierotti, last of the great English wax-doll craftsmen.

Rye Museum, Ypres Tower, Rye

This small museum in a thirteenth-century tower has a few Victorian dolls, old scrapbooks and early educational games.

ESSEX

Chelmsford Museum, Oatlands Park, Chelmsford
(tel: Chelmsford 53066)

A few toys are on show, including a mechanical violin-playing clown, tumblers, wooden soldiers on an extending scissors base, a zoetrope and a polyphon.

Colchester and Essex Museum, The Holly Trees,
Colchester (tel: Colchester 77475)

This interesting old house near the castle has a display of toys dating from the eighteenth century onwards, the earliest being board games, cup-and-ball and hornbooks. Among other Victorian toys are pedlar dolls (c. 1840-50) and a very well equipped late nineteenth-century dolls' house.

The Museum, Saffron Walden (tel: Saffron Walden 2494)

It is easy to miss this small museum near the church, which has some very interesting early toys among its exhibits: a doll's ivory knife and fork in a case (1750) and some good examples of dolls' clothes should not be overlooked. The dolls include one in Quaker dress (early nineteenth century, wax) and others dating from 1825 onwards. Also on show are a baby carriage, samplers, early children's books and some mid eighteenth-century baby caps.

Audley End House, Saffron Walden
Visitors to this palatial Jacobean mansion should look out for a large Georgian dolls' house on display there.

GLOUCESTERSHIRE

Snowshill Manor, near Broadway (tel: Broadway 2410)
This Cotswold manor-house, once the home of the late Mr Charles Wade, is still full of the innumerable treasures he collected. In a room on the top storey are dolls' houses, dolls, an ecclesiastical-looking Noah's ark and other Victorian toys. A box with fitted trays packed with hundreds of tiny Nuremberg wooden figures—people and animals—is miraculously complete. An adjoining room is devoted to wheeled vehicles of all sorts, from prams, bone-shakers and penny-farthings to perfect models of the distinctive wagons of each English county.

HEREFORD AND WORCESTER

City Museum and Art Gallery, Broad Street, Hereford (tel: Hereford 68121)
The collection includes about seventy dolls from c. 1800 to c. 1930, as well as Noah's arks, optical and mechanical toys, board games, soldiers, farm animals and a large furnished dolls' house of about 1860. As usual, most of the toys are Victorian, but the late eighteenth and early nineteenth centuries are quite well represented. There is normally a small display of toys and dolls on view at the branch Museum of Costume and Fine Arts at Churchill Gardens, Hereford.

Playthings Past Museum, Beaconwood, Beacon Lane, near Bromsgrove
Mrs Betty Cadbury's superb collection may be visited by parties of between twenty and thirty-five persons (it is regretted that the museum cannot be opened for individual visitors). Prior written application is essential. The toys and dolls here are of superlative quality, and there is a great deal to see. Soft plush cats which turn out to be nursery ninepins and a mechanical peacock with a spreading tail are two random memories, but every visitor will have a personal favourite from the 'magic world of childhood in a pre-plastic age'.

Eye Manor, Leominster (tel: Yarpole 244)
Mr and Mrs Christopher Sandford's Renaissance house is full of rare delights, but toy enthusiasts should particularly note the box of nineteenth-century games and the Victorian dolls' house with original carpets, curtains and wallpapers. There are eighteenth- and nineteenth-century dolls, including a pedlar woman with a baby, children's books, teddy-bears, cats and 'banbury' horses. A loan collection of fifty-six costume dolls made by Isabelle Beck and her mother, Hedy, displays the full sweep of fashion from 1150 to 1955.

Hereford and Worcester County Museum, Hartlebury Castle, Kidderminster (tel: Hartlebury 416)
The museum has a fine collection of toys: military, optical, mechanical, constructional and educational. There are three shops, two theatres, six Noah's arks, over two hundred dolls and three dolls' houses, though not all can be displayed together. Those who find Potter's stuffed animal tableaux appealing will also like *The Mouse's Card Party* (c. 1860).

Worcester City Museum and Art Gallery, Tudor House Museum, Friar Street, Worcester (tel: Worcester 25371)
A room full of toys includes a group of 1930s German bisque dolls from the Worcester Dolls' Hospital, some interesting dolls' house items (among them a nurse with twins), a biblical block puzzle, clockwork kitten (c. 1925), a Simon & Halbig 'Jutta' character doll (c. 1910). A small English wax doll, c. 1840, with black boots, is still in mint condition in its original box.

ISLE OF WIGHT

Arreton Manor, near Newport (tel: Arreton 255)
Besides much else of interest, this Jacobean manor-house has an extensive display of toys. There are about a hundred dolls, in superb condition and beautifully dressed, including French fashion dolls and English wax dolls (two being by the famous London maker Pierotti). As well as these, there is a wide variety of nineteenth-century playthings and nursery equipment; dolls' accessories, clothes, early kaleidoscopes, a miniature barrel organ, tea and dinner services are a few items chosen at random from this outstanding and well-arranged collection.

Lilliput Doll Museum, High Street, Brading (tel: Brading 231)
Another fine and comprehensive collection of period dolls, including one (c. 1790) dressed in a remnant of Queen Caroline's wedding gown, an unusual bisque doll presented by Queen Victoria to an estate employee's daughter at Christmas 1885, and a wax portrait doll of Lily Langtry; also felt and fabric dolls by Lenci and Dean's Rag Book Co. Ltd, famous in the field of English toys since 1903. Many other interesting toys are on show, and there is also a shop and dolls' hospital catering for collectors' needs.

Carisbrooke Castle Museum, Newport (tel: Newport 2107)
Visitors should look out for the Victorian dolls' house with several noteworthy pieces in it—an unusual birdcage, some ormolu clocks and a full dinner service.

Osborne House
The popularity of Queen Victoria's children did much to stimulate the toy trade, and many of their playthings, typifying all that was most lavish in the mid nineteenth-century nursery, are preserved in this favourite royal residence. Each child had its own initialled wheelbarrow and gardening tools, and the girls learned housewifery with specially scaled-down domestic equipment in the Swiss cottage: still to be seen are the kitchen range, the miniature tea and dinner services, bellows and a well-stocked grocer's shop.

KENT

The Royal Museum, High Street, Canterbury
(tel: Canterbury 52747)
A small but very interesting collection of dolls' house furniture should not be missed by anyone visiting the town.

Penshurst Place, near Tonbridge (tel: Penshurst 307)
In a converted outbuilding an interesting exhibition of toys has been arranged by Miss Yootha Rose, herself a collector and a talented toymaker. A group of wax dolls in bridal costume, a Pollock's toy theatre, colourful lotto cards, illustrated books and many other Victorian playthings are on view, as well as some examples of the beautiful wooden toys made by Miss Rose.

Rochester Museum, Eastgate House, Rochester
(tel: Medway 44176)

The toy section is small but includes such early items as cup-and-ball and a paper model stagecoach. A horse pulling a Kentish brick cart (c. 1870) was probably made locally, and among other dolls and toys is a dolls' house with a brass plate over the front door showing that it was 'Given to Constance H. S. Dahl by Uncle John, August 1882'. A variation on the pedlar doll theme is an 'industrious housewife' doll, loaded with pins, needles, buttons and other sewing necessities.

The Precinct Toy Collection, 38 Harnet Street, Sandwich

A wonderful toy museum, displaying the treasures its founder, Mrs Gandolfo, has been collecting all her life. The fleet of assorted Noah's arks is particularly impressive, but there is something to arouse nostalgia in everyone, from a wide range of magnificent period dolls and dolls' houses to much-loved animals, including a Pip, Squeak and Wilfred group.

Royal Tunbridge Wells Museum and Art Gallery, Civic
Centre, Tunbridge Wells (tel: Tunbridge Wells 26121)

The toy collection here is outstanding, with well over a hundred dolls of all kinds, a fine 1840 craftsman-made dolls' house with wonderful furniture, and a number of miniature shops and well-laden pedlars. The earliest toys include a model of a Kentish farm wagon made for the children at Lullingstone Castle in 1768, a peep-show dated 1815 and a strawwork ark. There are many different makes of toy soldiers, including 'flats' produced by Ernest Heinrichsen of Nuremberg in 1839, some with their original boxes. A zoetrope has been arranged to spin round continuously, showing how effective this optical device was; other unusual toys include a mechanical elephant from the Paris Exhibition of 1855, early steam locomotives, a German speaking picture book which emits animal noises, and movable wooden figures representing Lord Salisbury and Mr Gladstone wrestling with each other.

LANCASHIRE

Lancaster City Museum, Old Town Hall, Market Square,
Lancaster (tel: Lancaster 64637)

The museum's collection of toys is small and only occasionally on display, but individual items can be seen by prior arrangement. Toys and games date from the early nineteenth century to the recent past; there are mid nineteenth-century mechanical and later dolls.

The Judge's Lodging, Church Street, Lancaster

Dolls from the Barry Elder Collection will eventually be on display in this eighteenth-century house. Those who remember seeing this remarkable collection at Carr House, Bretherton, and before that in Hammersmith, will be pleased to know that much of it has survived intact, bought by the Lancashire County Museums Service.

Harris Museum and Art Gallery, Market Square, Preston
(tel: Preston 53989)

Lack of space limits the number of toys on show, but the museum has a collection of about one hundred and thirty dolls (including three wax dolls given in exchange for tea coupons in the 1880s), a very good selection of board games and some early educational games, as well as later games like Monopoly. The most popular exhibit is probably the charming dolls' house of about 1820.

LEICESTERSHIRE

Newarke Houses Museum, The Newarke, Leicester
(tel: Leicester 50988)

Another large and representative collection of Victorian dolls and toys. A lifelike wax portrait doll, representing a young girl with blue eyes and plaited hair, c. 1870, is exceptional.

LONDON

Bethnal Green Museum, Cambridge Heath Road, E2
(tel: 01-980 3204)

This museum, a branch of the Victoria and Albert, has an unrivalled collection of superb dolls, dolls' houses and toys. The earliest of the many baby-houses, dated 1673, was made in Nuremberg, as was the eighteenth-century model kitchen. There are also shops, pedlars, dinner services, rocking horses, early cut-out sheets for making rag dolls, and scores of other toys. A German Biberach catalogue of about 1836, with coloured illustrations, shows the wide variety of toys already available at that time.

The British Museum, Bloomsbury, WC1 (tel: 01-636 1555)
The toys on view are restricted to one or two Ancient Egyptian examples and one case containing a few from Greece and Rome.

Cuming Museum, Walworth Road, SE17 (tel: 01-703 3324)
A very small collection, but interesting for the display of cheap wooden toys bought at Bartholomew Fair in 1849— among other things a dog, a cow on wheels, 'big dipper' and a lady-up-a-stick. There is also a wax doll bought at Ascot races in the same year.

Geffrye Museum, Kingsland Road, Shoreditch, E2 (tel: 01-739 8368)
Not far from the Bethnal Green treasure-house, this museum has a few toys and pieces of nursery equipment on show as part of the furnishings of various period rooms.

Gunnersbury Park Museum, W3 (tel: 01-992 2247)
A few Victorian dolls and two dolls' houses are displayed in this former home of the Rothschilds.

Horniman Museum, Forest Hill, SE23 (tel: 01-699 2339)
An ethnographical museum, with folk toys and dolls from all over the world. The exhibits are quite different from the usual collections of Victorian toys and include an Egyptian earthenware rattle (c. 1360 B.C.), painted Easter eggs from the Balkans and balls of plaited palm, whistles, tops and kites from the Far East. (British kite-flyers, incidentally, will no doubt be surprised to learn that an official regulation, Article 62 of the Air Navigation Order 1970, prohibits kites within three miles of any aerodrome and also restricts them to a height of 200 feet in any other part of the United Kingdom.)

Museum of London, London Wall, London, EC2
A small part of the important toy collection of the old London Museum, formerly at Kensington Palace, is now on view at this new museum, which combines the collections of the former London and Guildhall Museums.

Pollock's Toy Museum, 1 Scala Street, W1 (tel: 01-636 3452)
In 1955 Mrs Marguerite Fawdry bought up all the copper-plates and prints which had formed the stock-in-trade of the original Pollock's Toy Theatre Shop, and from this beginning grew her ever-expanding museum not only of toy theatres but of all sorts of other playthings. Several very informative

Figures from Pollock's Toy Theatre.

booklets are on sale at the museum, besides everything necessary for making a toy theatre, traditional gingerbread and Happy Families cards, and other nostalgic items.

Times Remembered Doll and Toy Museum, The Coach House, Syon Park, Brentford (tel: 01-560 8776)

An outstanding and very informative collection in a beautiful setting. The visitor will learn much from the magnificent dolls on show, but more unusual displays – for example a case devoted to embossed paper 'scraps' and another filled with snow babies from bygone Christmas cakes – indicate the wide variety of items now collected by toy enthusiasts.

Victoria and Albert Museum, South Kensington, SW7 (tel: 01-589 6371)

Some very well-preserved eighteenth-century dolls are on display including the celebrated 'Lord and Lady Clapham', bought for the museum for £16,000. The library contains a great many useful reference books giving information about toys, and some rare children's books like *The Girl's Own Toymaker* (1860) and Gordon Graig's *Book of Penny Toys* (1899). Booklets on toys, dolls, and dolls' houses (illustrated with photographs of exhibits at Bethnal Green) are available at the bookstall, together with replicas of early cotton cut-out doll sheets and some attractive posters.

GREATER MANCHESTER

Salford Museum and Art Gallery, Peel Park, Salford (tel: 061-736 2649)

A selection of toys has been arranged in one of the shop windows in the period 'street'. There is an early Victorian toy theatre, a straw-work ark of the prisoner-of-war type, diabolo, tops, magic lanterns, dolls, books and other playthings, mainly nineteenth-century but with earlier and later examples too.

NORFOLK

Museum of Social History, 27 King Street, King's Lynn (tel: King's Lynn 5001)

One room is devoted to toys; there are a number of interesting dolls, and an impressive Victorian dolls' house with well-documented local connections.

Strangers' Hall, Charing Cross, Norwich (tel: Norwich 22233)

A fine collection of dolls and toys, including some well furnished dolls' houses, a full-size Punch and Judy booth, tinplate toys and a variety of games. A museum booklet, *Teaching Toys* by Rachel Young, is available.

NORTHUMBERLAND

Wallington Hall, Cambo, Morpeth (tel: Scots Gap 283)

The nursery at Wallington has been arranged to look as if a family of children had just left it. There are Victorian dolls, a very unusual horse-tricycle propelled by handles in the neck instead of by pedals, a dolls' dinner service, a toy farm and children's books. Most of these, and many more besides, belonged to the Trevelyan family and have always been at Wallington. Some remarkable dolls' houses are displayed separately: one, dated 1892, has thirty-six rooms, running water and a lift, about a thousand pieces of furniture and fifty dolls.

NORTH YORKSHIRE

Royal Pump Room Museum, Harrogate (tel: Harrogate 503340)

The exhibits are changed from time to time; the interesting collection of dolls and toys includes some later examples such as Dinky cars and a 1930s dolls' house, as well as a Montanari wax fashion doll, a very fully furnished Victorian dolls' house and a miniature hose cart for fire-fighting.

The Castle Museum, York (tel: York 53611)

This is an outstanding collection, with a great many dolls and toys displayed. The Heslington baby-house, possibly designed by Sir John Vanbrugh and certainly one of the oldest in the country, should be specially noted. The exhibits range from large rocking horses and elaborate toy theatres to bygone sweets.

OXFORDSHIRE

The Rotunda, Grove House, 44 Iffley Turn, Oxford

Mrs Graham Greene's private collection of dolls' houses, in its specially built rotunda, is open to the public on summer Sunday afternoons. These exquisite eighteenth- and nineteenth-century houses, with their abundance of contemporary miniature furnishings, are intended to appeal to grown-ups, and children under sixteen are not admitted. Tiny newspapers, books and other things liable to get overlooked inside a dolls' house are arranged in a separate showcase.

SOMERSET

Beckington Pram, Dolls and Toys Museum, The Old Manse, Beckington, near Frome (tel: Beckington 531)

The seventeenth-century mansion houses a good collection of toys, dolls in period costume and baby carriages.

Memorial Hall, High Street, Dunster

A surprisingly little-known collection of over seven hundred dolls, the earliest dating from the eighteenth century, collected by the late Molly Hardwick. There is also a dolls' house.

Somerset County Museum, The Castle, Taunton (tel: Taunton 3451 or 7591)

The toy section consists of about twenty dolls, plus an eighteenth-century dolls' four-poster bed and a group of miniature dolls; other toys are in store.

SOUTH YORKSHIRE

Museum and Art Gallery, Chequer Road, Doncaster
(tel: Doncaster 62095)
    Two shop-window-type displays show Victorian and Edwardian dolls, a dolls' house, toy theatre, board games, ships and other playthings.

Cusworth Hall Museum, Cusworth Lane, Doncaster
(tel: Doncaster 61842)
    The Children's Room contains a collection of toys.

Bishops' House, Meersbrook Park, Sheffield
(tel: Sheffield 57701)
    This is a late fifteenth-century timber-framed domestic building, with later additions. There is a children's room with a constantly changing display of toys dating from 1800 onwards.

STAFFORDSHIRE

Museum of Childhood and Costume, Blithfield Hall, Rugeley
(tel: Dapple Heath 249)
    Nancy Lady Bagot's very large collection of dolls, toys, theatres, nursery equipment and children's costume is mainly Victorian but includes some eighteenth-century examples too. Punch and Judy figures, a toy barrel organ complete with monkey, model stagecoaches, a two-seater rocking horse and early children's books are just a few of the interesting things displayed in the nursery rooms.

Staffordshire County Museum and Mansion House,
Shugborough (tel: Little Haywood 388)
    There is a great deal to see here, but a small group of dolls in the museum should not be overlooked.

SUFFOLK

Ipswich Museum, High Street, Ipswich (tel: Ipswich 211211)
    Ipswich possesses a considerable number of interesting toys and dolls, including about forty wax dolls, a wide variety of dolls' house furniture and accessories, a sand toy, farmyards, lead soldiers, clockwork toys, optical toys, games and

children's picture books. However, intending visitors should note that they are stored during the year and only brought out at Christmas time and until the end of January. The only toys on permanent display are a few items in the Nursery at Christchurch Mansion, Christchurch Park.

SURREY

Educational Museum, Haslemere (tel: Haslemere 2112)
There is a late Victorian dolls' house and a small collection of dolls, including some eighteenth-century ones and a charming wedding group of five late nineteenth-century wax dolls.

WARWICKSHIRE

Warwick Doll Museum, Oken's House, Castle Street, Warwick
It is impossible to pick out individual items from the superb collection of high-quality dolls and toys which fills this Elizabethan house, and visitors should allow themselves plenty of time to appreciate its countless treasures. Besides magnificent dolls there are beds, perambulators, dolls' houses and—as at the Rotunda in Oxford—special displays of exquisite miniature objects.

WEST MIDLANDS

City Museum and Art Gallery, Birmingham 3 (tel: 021-236 2834)
This museum houses the Pinto Collection of Wooden Bygones, between six and seven thousand objects made from wood, ranging from a carved peach stone to a fire engine, and from the Middle Ages to the present day. It includes many interesting toys, puzzles, games and pieces of miniature furniture; a hornbook, usually strictly educational, is here combined with a rattle and has a doll's head carved at the top.

Aston Hall, Trinity Road, Birmingham (tel: 021-327 0062)
One room arranged as a Victorian nursery has typical toys and children's furniture—a pedlar doll, rocking horse, miniature organ and other playthings.

63

The Coventry Toy Museum, Much Park Street, Coventry
An interesting private collection, on display in one of the City's few remaining medieval buildings.

Bantock House Museum, Bantock Park, Wolverhampton (tel: Wolverhampton 24548)
One of Wolverhampton Corporation's museums, Bantock House has a good display of tourist, ethnographic and folk dolls to complement its collection of conventional play dolls. Most types are represented – early wooden examples, papier maché, wax, porcelain, rag, bisque, celluloid and composition. There are pieces of miniature furniture too, and prams, games and other toys. An excellent catalogue, *English and Foreign Dolls c. 1780 to c. 1950,* and a coloured poster are on sale.

WEST SUSSEX

Potter's Museum of Curiosity, 6 High Street, Arundel (tel: Arundel 882420)
Devotees of the old Potter's Museum at Bramber will be relieved that its unique exhibits were rescued intact, and Mr James Cartland has re-established them in an appropriate setting at Arundel. Although strictly speaking they are not toys, these stuffed animal tableaux are so toy-like in inspiration and feeling that they cannot be left out of this list. Walter Potter, taxidermist extraordinary, was born in 1835 and spent most of his life creating nursery-rhyme groups of kittens, rabbits, squirrels and other small animals. His masterpiece was suggested by the *Death of Cock Robin,* but the *Kittens' Wedding* (all participants are sumptuously dressed), the *Rabbits' School* and the *House That Jack Built* are all works of imaginative genius. A selection of more conventional period toys has recently been added to the museum.

Uppark, South Harting, near Petersfield
The famous baby-house, built about 1730, accompanied its original owner when she came to Uppark as a bride. It has a fine Palladian facade topped by seven statues, and underneath the house is an arcaded stand intended for model carriages. On Connoisseurs' Day, once a month, the dolls' house is opened up and visitors can appreciate to the full its nine panelled rooms furnished with everything a full-size Georgian house would have had.

The Priest House, West Hoathly (tel: Sharpthorne 479)
Displayed with other bygones are about thirty-five Victorian and Edwardian dolls, and ship and other models.

Worthing Museum and Art Gallery, Chapel Road, Worthing (tel: Worthing 39189)
This is another outstanding collection, and only a small part can be shown at any one time. Most toys dating from about 1750 to 1910 are represented, and there is a large collection of educational toys and games. The extensive doll collection is admirably described and photographed in the museum's doll catalogue and includes *The History of Little Fanny* (1810), a rare cut-out paper doll combined with a story book.

WEST YORKSHIRE

Bolling Hall Museum, Bowling Hall Road, Bradford (tel: Bradford 23057)
A small collection of Victorian and later toys is on display.

Tolson Memorial Museum, Ravensknowle Park, Huddersfield (tel: Huddersfield 30591)
This museum has a good selection of playthings, especially of clockwork and 'penny' toys and optical toys. Dolls and dolls' furniture are also shown.

Abbey House Museum, Kirkstall, Leeds (tel: Leeds 55821)
Only a fifth of this enormous collection can be shown at any one time, and displays are frequently changed. Almost every sort of toy and game from the eighteenth century to the present day is represented, and a selection of modern toys is added each year. Rarities include a mid nineteenth-century cast iron paddle steamer, an 1890 French omnibus and *Reed's Sunday Toy*—a set of blocks printed with scriptural texts from which a church could be constructed.

Nostell Priory, Wakefield
The very impressive mid eighteenth-century baby-house is described on pages 10 and 11.

City Museum, Wood Street, Wakefield (tel: Wakefield 61767)
A shop window display contains, among other eighteenth-

and nineteenth-century toys, eleven ventriloquists' dolls, a magic lantern with slides, and a child's sewing machine. There are several model steam engines, one of which won a first award at the Wakefield Industrial Exhibition of 1865.

WILTSHIRE

Salisbury and South Wiltshire Museum, St Ann Street, Salisbury (tel: Salisbury 4465)
A few dolls and toys are shown.

Longleat House, Warminster (tel: Maiden Bradley 303)
The Longleat dolls' house was made in 1870 for the daughters of the fourth Marquess of Bath and was modelled on a house in Ireland.

SCOTLAND

Museum of Childhood, 34 High Street, Edinburgh (tel: 031-556 5447)
A superb museum covering all aspects of childhood—games, toys, books, health and education. As well as the more usual luxury toys there are displays of cracker contents, a pre-war twopenny bar of chocolate (an immense block) and a doll made by a slum child from a wrapped-up shoe. Meticulous labelling and dating add greatly to the value of the collection, and for this and much else all toy enthusiasts must thank that untiring chronicler, Mr Patrick Murray.

WALES

Penrhyn Castle, Bangor
A large collection of dolls from all parts of the world has gradually been built up since the early 1950s. A few date back to about 1820, and there are some good mid nineteenth-century English wax dolls. Portrait figures of First World War leaders, including Kitchener and French, and other uniformed dolls of c. 1940 make an interesting group. Various Victorian and Edwardian toys are displayed with the dolls.

Welsh Folk Museum, St Fagans, Cardiff (tel: Cardiff 561357)
The museum has a miscellany of Victorian toys and dolls, musical boxes and games of every description from chess to spillikins.

Llandudno Doll Museum and Model Railway Exhibition, Llandudno (tel: Llandudno 76312)

There are over a thousand dolls here, of all kinds, with much to interest both children and adults. The model railway room caters especially for boys. A rare 'blue scarf' doll (with moulded headdress) and a black velvet Felix the Cat are picked at random.

Museum of Childhood, Water Street, Menai Bridge (tel: Menai Bridge 712001)

An unusually varied collection, including all sorts of nursery paraphernalia. There are toy savings boxes, dolls, educational toys, games, trains, cars and clockwork models, music boxes, polyphons and magic lanterns. One room has a particularly attractive display of pottery and glass either depicting or used by children – 'Mary Gregory' glass, and a wide assortment of tiles, plates and mugs.

BIBLIOGRAPHY

Peter Bull: *Bear With Me* (Hutchinson, 1969)

Betty Cadbury: *Playthings Past* (David & Charles, 1976)

Robert Culff: *The World of Toys* (Hamlyn, 1969)

Leslie Daiken: *Children's Toys throughout the Ages* (Batsford, 1953)

Kay Desmonde: *Dolls and Dolls' Houses* (Letts, 1972)

Faith Eaton: *Dolls in Colour* (Blandford, 1975)

Antonia Fraser: *A History of Toys* (Weidenfeld & Nicolson, 1966)

K. E. Fritzsch and M. Bachmann: *An Illustrated History of Toys* (Abbey Library, 1966)

Lesley Gordon: *Peepshow Into Paradise* (Harrap, 1953)

Vivien Greene: *English Dolls' Houses of the Eighteenth and Nineteenth Centuries* (Batsford, 1955)

Vivien Greene: *Family Dolls' Houses* (Bell, 1973)

Mary Hillier: *Pageant of Toys* (Elek, 1965)

Mary Hillier: *Dolls and Dollmakers* (Weidenfeld & Nicolson, 1968)

Mary Hillier: *Automata and Mechanical Toys* (Jupiter Books, 1976)

Jean Latham: *Doll's Houses: A Personal Choice* (A. & C. Black, 1969)

Patrick Murray: *Toys* (Studio Vista, 1968)

George Speaight: *The History of English Toy Theatre* (Studio Vista, 1969)

Gwen White: *European and American Dolls* (Batsford, 1966)

Gwen White: *Antique Toys and their Background* (Batsford, 1971).

INDEX

Discovering Antique Maps
Discovering Archaeology in Denmark
Discovering Archaeology in England and Wales
Discovering Avon
Discovering Backgammon
Discovering Banknotes
Discovering Battlefields of Scotland
Discovering Beekeeping
Discovering Bells and Bellringing
Discovering Bird Song
Discovering Bird Watching
Discovering Brasses and Brassrubbing
Discovering British Cavalry Regiments
Discovering British Ponies
Discovering the Burns Country
Discovering Cambridgeshire
Discovering Canals
Discovering Castle Combe
Discovering Castles in England and Wales
Discovering Cathedrals
Discovering Chapels and Meeting Houses
Discovering Cheshire
Discovering Chess
Christmas Customs and Folklore
Discovering Church Architecture
Discovering Churches
Discovering Corn Dollies
Discovering Country Crafts
Discovering Craft of the Inland Waterways
Discovering Derbyshire and the Peak District
Discovering Edged Weapons
Discovering English Folk Dance
Discovering English Furniture
Discovering English Literary Associations
Discovering Essex
Discovering Famous Battles: The Peninsular War
Discovering Farm Museums and Farm Parks
Discovering the Folklore and Customs of Love and Marriage
Discovering the Folklore of Plants
Discovering French and German Military Uniforms
Discovering Garden Insects
Gardening for the Handicapped
Discovering Hall-marks on English Silver
Discovering Hampshire
Discovering Herbs
Discovering Hill Figures
Discovering Horse Brasses
Discovering Horse-drawn Carriages
Discovering Horse-drawn Commercial Vehicles
Discovering Industrial Archaeology and History
Discovering Kent
Discovering Kings and Queens
Discovering Lakeland
Discovering Lancashire
Discovering Leicestershire and Rutland
Discovering Lincolnshire
Discovering London for Children
Discovering London's Canals
Discovering London Street Names
Discovering London Villages
Discovering Lost Canals